W9-ACM-238

SPARKS OF LIFE

Chemical Elements that Make Life Possible

PHOSPHORUS

by

Jean F. Blashfield

 RAINTREE
STECK-VAUGHN
PUBLISHERS

A Harcourt Company

Austin · New York
www.steck-vaughn.com

Special thanks to our technical consultant,
Philip T. Johns, Ph.D.,
University of Wisconsin–Whitewater, Wisconsin

Development: Books Two, Delavan, Wisconsin
    Graphics: Krueger Graphics, Janesville, Wisconsin
    Interior Design: Peg Esposito
    Photo Research and Indexing: Margie Benson

Raintree Steck-Vaughn Publisher's Staff:
    Publishing Director: Walter Kossmann   Project Editor: Frank Tarsitano
    Design Manager: Joyce Spicer   Electronic Production: Scott Melcer

Library of Congress Cataloging-in-Publication Data:
Blashfield, Jean F.
    Phosphorus / by Jean F. Blashfield.
        p. cm. — (Sparks of life)
    Includes bibliographical references and index.
    ISBN 0-7398-3450-9
        1. Phosphorus--Juvenile literature. 2. Phosphorus--Physiological aspects--Juvenile literature. [1. Phosphorus.] I. Title.

    QD181.P1. B53 2001
    545'.712--dc21   00-045689

Printed and bound in the United States
1 2 3 4 5 6 7 8 9 LB 05 04 03 02 01

PHOTO CREDITS: Agricultural Research Service, USDA 45; Archive Photos 26; B.I.F.C. cover; ©Dr. Jeremy Burgess/Science Photo Library 57; ©David Cavagnaro/Peter Arnold Inc. 25, 27; ©1997, CRNI/Science Photo Library/Custom Medical Stock Photo 44; ©Kevin & Betty Collins/Visuals Unlimited 22; ©David Cornwell/Pacific Stock 30; ©Jeff J. Daley/Visuals Unlimited 31; ©Darodents/Pacific Stock 18; ©David Dennis/Earth Scenes 49; Derby Museum & Art Gallery 11; ©Eastcott/Momatiuk/Earth Scenes 24; Dr. Joanna Fowler/ Brookhaven National Laboratory 56; ©Stanley L. Gibbs/Peter Arnold Inc. 41; ©Jeff Greenberg/Visuals Unlimited 38; ©Dr. Michael Klein/Peter Arnold Inc. 40; ©Tom Pantages 37; ©Alfred Pasieka/Peter Arnold Inc. 34; ©Darrell C.H. Plowes 28; ©Jo Prater/Visuals Unlimited 16; ©Harry J. Przekop, Stock Shop/Medichrome cover; ©Mark A. Schneider/The National Audubon Society Collect/Photo Researchers 53; ©1991 Science Photo Library/Customer Medical Stock Photo 32; ©Tek Image/Science Photo Library 14; ©R. Toms/Earth Scenes 47; ©Rich Treptow/Visuals Unlimited 13; ©George Whiteley/The National Audubon Society Collection/Photo Researchers 20; ©George J. Wilder/Visuals Unlimited 29

CONTENTS

Periodic Table of the Elements

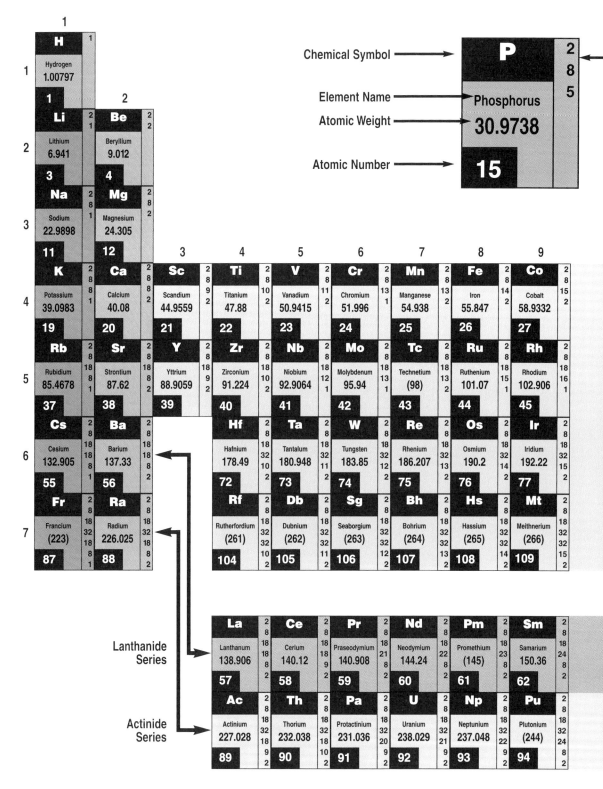

Number of electrons in each shell, beginning with the K shell, top.

See next page for explanations.

18

He 2
Helium
4.0026
2

13	14	15	16	17	
B 2 3	**C** 2 4	**N** 2 5	**O** 2 6	**F** 2 7	**Ne** 2 8
Boron 10.81	Carbon 12.011	Nitrogen 14.0067	Oxygen 15.9994	Fluorine 18.9984	Neon 20.179
5	6	7	8	9	10
Al 2 8 3	**Si** 2 8 4	**P** 2 8 5	**S** 2 8 6	**Cl** 2 8 7	**Ar** 2 8 8
Aluminum 26.9815	Silicon 28.0855	Phosphorus 30.9738	Sulfur 32.06	Chlorine 35.453	Argon 39.948
13	14	15	16	17	18

10	11	12	13	14	15	16	17	18
Ni 2 8 16 2	**Cu** 2 8 18 1	**Zn** 2 8 18 2	**Ga** 2 8 18 3	**Ge** 2 8 18 4	**As** 2 8 18 5	**Se** 2 8 18 6	**Br** 2 8 18 7	**Kr** 2 8 18 8
Nickel 58.69	Copper 63.546	Zinc 65.39	Gallium 69.72	Germanium 72.59	Arsenic 74.9216	Selenium 78.96	Bromine 79.904	Krypton 83.80
28	29	30	31	32	33	34	35	36
Pd 2 8 18 18	**Ag** 2 8 18 18 1	**Cd** 2 8 18 18 2	**In** 2 8 18 18 3	**Sn** 2 8 18 18 4	**Sb** 2 8 18 18 5	**Te** 2 8 18 18 6	**I** 2 8 18 18 7	**Xe** 2 8 18 18 8
Palladium 106.42	Silver 107.868	Cadmium 112.41	Indium 114.82	Tin 118.71	Antimony 121.75	Tellurium 127.6	Iodine 126.905	Xenon 131.29
46	47	48	49	50	51	52	53	54
Pt 2 8 18 32 17 1	**Au** 2 8 18 32 18 1	**Hg** 2 8 18 32 18 2	**Tl** 2 8 18 32 18 3	**Pb** 2 8 18 32 18 4	**Bi** 2 8 18 32 18 5	**Po** 2 8 18 32 18 6	**At** 2 8 18 32 18 7	**Rn** 2 8 18 32 18 8
Platinum 195.08	Gold 196.967	Mercury 200.59	Thallium 204.383	Lead 207.2	Bismuth 208.98	Polonium (209)	Astatine (210)	Radon (222)
78	79	80	81	82	83	84	85	86
(Uun) 2 8 18 32 32 17 1	**(Unu)** 2 8 18 32 32 18 1	**(Uub)** 2 8 18 32 32 18 2						
(Ununnilium) (269)	(Unununium) (272)	(Ununbium) (277)						
110	111	112						

COLOR KEYS

Alkali Metals | Transition Metals | Nonmetals | Metalloids | Lanthanide Series
Alkaline Earth Metals | Other Metals | Noble Gases | Actinide Series

Eu 2 8 18 25 8 2	**Gd** 2 8 18 25 9 2	**Tb** 2 8 18 27 8 2	**Dy** 2 8 18 28 8 2	**Ho** 2 8 18 29 8 2	**Er** 2 8 18 30 8 2	**Tm** 2 8 18 31 8 2	**Yb** 2 8 18 32 8 2	**Lu** 2 8 18 32 9 2
Europium 151.96	Gadolinium 157.25	Terbium 158.925	Dysprosium 162.50	Holmium 164.93	Erbium 167.26	Thulium 168.934	Ytterbium 173.04	Lutetium 174.967
63	64	65	66	67	68	69	70	71
Am 2 8 18 32 25 8 2	**Cm** 2 8 18 32 25 9 2	**Bk** 2 8 18 32 26 9 2	**Cf** 2 8 18 32 28 8 2	**Es** 2 8 18 32 29 8 2	**Fm** 2 8 18 32 30 8 2	**Md** 2 8 18 32 31 8 2	**No** 2 8 18 32 32 8 2	**Lr** 2 8 18 32 32 9 2
Americium (243)	Curium (247)	Berkelium (247)	Californium (251)	Einsteinium (254)	Fermium (257)	Mendelevium (258)	Nobelium (259)	Lawrencium (260)
95	96	97	98	99	100	101	102	103

A Guide to the Periodic Table

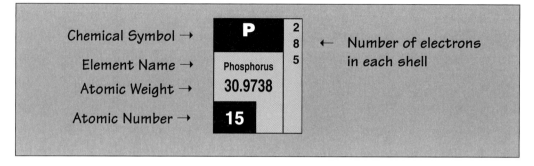

Chemical Symbol → **P**   2 8 5   ← Number of electrons in each shell

Element Name → Phosphorus

Atomic Weight → 30.9738

Atomic Number → 15

Symbol = an abbreviation of an element name, agreed on by members of the International Union of Pure and Applied Chemistry. The idea to use symbols was started by a Swedish chemist, Jöns Jakob Berzelius, about 1814. Note that the elements with numbers 110, 111, and 112, which were "discovered" in 1996, have not yet been given official names.

Atomic number = the number of protons (particles with a positive electrical charge) in the nucleus of an atom of an element; also equal to the number of electrons (particles with a negative electrical charge) found in the shells, or rings, of an atom that does not have an electrical charge.

Atomic weight = the weight of an element compared to carbon. When the Periodic Table was first developed, hydrogen was used as the standard. It was given an atomic weight of 1, but that created some difficulties, and in 1962, the standard was changed to carbon-12, which is the most common form of the element carbon, with an atomic weight of 12.

The Periodic Table on pages 4 and 5 shows the atomic weight of carbon as 12.011 because an atomic weight is an average of the weights, or masses, of all the different naturally occurring forms of an atom. Each form, called an isotope, has a different number of neutrons (uncharged particles) in the nucleus. Most elements have several isotopes, but chemists assume that any two samples of an element are made up of the same mixture of isotopes and thus have the same mass, or weight.

Electron shells = regions surrounding the nucleus of an atom in which the electrons move. Historically, electron shells have been described as orbits similar to a planet's orbit. But actually they are whole areas of a specific energy level, in which certain electrons vibrate and move around. The shell closest to the nucleus, the K shell, can contain only 2 electrons. The K shell has the lowest energy level, and it is very hard to break its electrons away. The second shell, L, can contain only 8 electrons. Others may contain up to 32 electrons. The outer shell, in which chemical reactions occur, is called the valence shell.

Periods = horizontal rows of elements in the Periodic Table. A period contains all the elements with the same number of orbital shells of electrons. Note that the actinide and lanthanide (or rare earth) elements shown in rows below the main table really belong within the table, but it is not regarded as practical to print such a wide table as would be required.

Groups = vertical columns of elements in the Periodic Table; also called families. A group contains all elements that naturally have the same number of electrons in the outermost shell or orbital of the atom. Elements in a group tend to behave in similar ways.

Group 1 = alkali metals: very reactive and so never found in nature in their pure form. Bright, soft metals, they have one valence electron and, like all metals, conduct both electricity and heat.

Group 2 = alkaline earth metals: also very reactive and thus don't occur pure in nature. Harder and denser than alkali metals, they have two valence electrons that easily combine with other chemicals.

Groups 3–12 = transition metals: the great mass of metals, with a variable number of electrons; can exist in pure form.

Groups 13–17 = transition metals, metalloids, and nonmetals. Metalloids possess some characteristics of metals and some of nonmetals. Unlike metals and metalloids, nonmetals do not conduct electricity

Group 18 = noble, or rare, gases: in general, these nonmetallic gaseous elements do not react with other elements because their valence shells are full.

ATOMS
AGLOW

What a wondrous thing it was to see something glow in the dark without any fire! People of long ago knew several materials that naturally glowed in the dark. They often called such materials *phosphorus,* which means "bearer of light" in Greek. The morning star—later known to be the planet Venus—was called Phosphoros by the Greeks.

Today, we know that phosphorus is a chemical element, a substance that cannot be broken down into different substances. Like many elements, it is poisonous, or toxic, to humans in its pure, elemental form, but it is an essential element for all living things. It is a **macronutrient**, one of eleven elements needed in fairly large quantities for human life. Every single cell of the human body contains phosphorus, as does everything we eat—plant or animal.

Element Number 15

Phosphorus has the chemical symbol P. Its atomic number is 15, which indicates that it has 15 protons, or particles with a positive electrical charge, in its nucleus, or center. The 15 protons in a phosphorus atom are balanced by 15 electrons, which have a negative electrical charge. Electrons move around the nucleus in regions called orbits or shells.

In addition to the protons, the nucleus also includes neutrons, which have no electrical charge. Atoms of natural phosphorus have 16 neutrons, giving P atoms an atomic weight, or mass number, of 31 (15 protons plus 16 neutrons). Phosphorus-31 (P-31) is the natural isotope, or form, of the element. All isotopes of an element occupy the same place on the Periodic Table (*isotope* means "same place"). They have the same atomic number (number of protons) but different mass numbers.

Artificial isotopes are created by bombarding natural ones with neutrons, a process that changes the number of neutrons. Phosphorus isotopes range from P-29 to P-34. When all the isotopes are considered together, phosphorus has an atomic weight, or mass, of 30.9738.

In the Periodic Table of the Elements, phosphorus is located in Period, or row, 3, which indicates that it has three electron shells. The first shell, closest to the nucleus, holds two electrons, the second holds eight, and the third, or outer, shell contains five. However, that third shell is capable of holding 18 electrons. Since that shell is not complete, phosphorus reacts with other elements to complete it. As we'll see shortly, atoms of the kind of phosphorus called white phosphorus will react with each other to form molecules of pure phosphorus.

Phosphorus is a nonmetal in Group 15 (sometimes called Group Va) of the Periodic Table, along with nitrogen (N, element #7), arsenic (As, #33), antimony (Sb [for the Latin word *stibium*],

#51), and bismuth (Bi, #83). Each of these elements also has five electrons in its outer, or valence, shell.

Molecules of Phosphorus

You may know that the air we breathe contains oxygen (O, element #8) molecules, not lone oxygen atoms. The atoms unite with each other to form diatomic, or two-atomed, molecules, usually written O_2. The most common form of phosphorus does the same kind of thing, although its atoms form molecules made up of four atoms.

Even if a valence shell can hold eighteen electrons, as the outer shell of phosphorus can, it will be stable, or not very reactive, if it has eight electrons in it. Since a phosphorus atom has five electrons in its valence shell, it shares one electron with each of three other atoms. The four atoms of a phosphorus molecule, P_4, form a shape called a tetrahedron.

In a P_4 molecule, each atom shares an electron with each of the other three atoms. They form a tetrahedron.

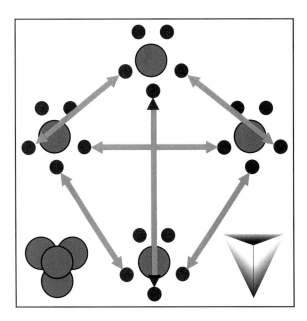

Finding the Fire

Phosphorus was discovered by a German physician and alchemist by the name of Hennig Brand in 1669. Alchemy was the forerunner of chemistry. Alchemists combined science with philosophy, religion, and a bit of magic. They were fascinated by the way differ-

Hennig Brand shown as "The Alchemist in Search of the Philosopher's Stone," in a painting by Wright of Derby

ent materials could be changed, hoping to find a way to turn cheap metals into gold (Au, for *aurum,* element #79).

Most alchemists were very curious about all the chemical substances they saw around them, and Brand was no different. Something prompted him to boil down huge quantities of urine. Finally, after long days of tending the fire to keep the liquid boiling, he boiled, strained, powdered, and otherwise treated the material that was left over, until a white, waxy crust was left in the bottom of the pot. Brand went down in history as the first person to discover an element whose existence of which had not even been suspected.

Brand had no idea then that the element was poisonous or could catch fire all on its own. He found out about the ease with which it burned, though, by carelessly breathing on some of the white, waxy material. It burst into flame, seriously burning his hand before he could get it out of the flames.

Amazingly, the material that Brand isolated glowed in the dark. He called it *phosphorus*, as a "bearer of light." Pure phosphorus appears to glow because atoms on the surface of the element are reacting with oxygen, or burning, in the air around it. For that same reason, materials that glow are often referred to as *phosphorescent*, even if they don't include phosphorus. The material used in the coating inside a TV screen is called a phosphor, for example, because it continues to give off light for a brief time after it has been struck by the rays in the TV tube. These phosphors are generally made of zinc sulfide, a chemical made of a combination of zinc (Zn, element #30) and sulfur (S, #16). Some phosphors used to coat the inside of fluorescent lights actually do contain some phosphorus, however.

As word of Brand's new, glowing element spread, experimenters (it was too early to call them chemists) became excited. Because Brand kept his process for making phosphorus secret, though, some other people tried to claim credit for the discovery. But mathematician, philosopher, and scientist Gottfried Leibniz, a friend of Brand's, made sure that Brand later received a regular salary from a German duke for revealing how to make "cold fire."

Among the Europeans fascinated by the glowing substance was German chemist Andreas S. Marggraf, who experimented with the material about 1740, though he still didn't know what it was. He showed that the material existed in many of the vegetables people eat.

It wasn't until the late eighteenth century that Antoine Lavoisier, the French founder of modern chemistry, proved that Brand's chemical was, in fact, an element. Gradually, researchers found that virtually all living things, both plant and animal, contain phosphorus. It is also found in many of Earth's minerals.

Many Faces of Phosphorus

Phosphorus is an element with many faces. It exists in at least three forms, or allotropes. And each of the main allotropes also has several forms.

The white, waxy substance obtained by Brand and others is extremely poisonous. Elemental white phosphorus smells rather like garlic. It ignites spontaneously with the oxygen in air at temperatures above 88°F (31°C).

White phosphorus (left), kept in water to keep it from exploding, and red powdered phosphorus (right)

When white phosphorus is heated in a closed chamber where oxygen cannot get to it, it changes to a deep-red powder called red phosphorus. This form is not toxic, nor does it flare up readily. Red phosphorus will also form if white phosphorus is exposed to sunlight.

The great Swedish chemist Jöns Jakob Berzelius, who worked in the early 1800s, was the first to say that red phosphorus was a variation of the element itself and not a compound formed with air, as most scientists thought. This idea was confirmed experimentally by Austrian chemist Anton von

Schrötter in 1848. Von Schrötter is credited with discovering this allotrope.

A third allotrope is black phosphorus, which looks like coal. Denser and more stable than red or white phosphorus, it is produced by putting white phosphorus under great pressure. This process uses a chemical containing mercury (Hg [for *hydrargyrum*], element #80). The mercury is a catalyst—it takes part in the change but is not changed itself. Black phosphorus will not form unless there is a crystal of black phosphorus in the container to act as a "seed."

Setting Fire

Matches were made of phosphorus as early as 1851. Von Shrötter made the first matches of red phosphorus, but his inventions were difficult to light.

Matches burn because the heat caused by rubbing the match head against a rough surface causes the chemicals in the head to ignite. The head of a match that can be struck against any rough surface is usually made of a mixture of chemicals. That mixture includes red phosphorus and potassium chlorate, $KClO_3$. (Potassium is K [for *kalium*], element #19; chlorine is Cl, #17.) These strike-anywhere matches can be dangerous because they can be ignited accidentally.

The solution to that problem was the safety match, which will ignite only when struck against a special surface, which is locat-

The first flare of a match ignites a layer of phosphorus trisulphide on the tip. Other chemicals take over.

ed on the matchbox. A safety match has no phosphorus in the match head. Instead, the phosphorus is in the striking strip on the matchbox. When the head of the match is struck against the striking strip, oxygen is released. Oxygen and phosphorus cause a spark that ignites the chemicals in the match head long enough to set other chemicals and the wood or cardboard of the match on fire.

Red phosphorus is not completely stable and will ignite if struck. The "ammunition" used in toy cap guns contains red phosphorus. The striking of the hammer on the flat surface the caps move across ignites the phosphorus, making it explode with a loud popping sound.

Obtaining the Element

White phosphorus—also called yellow phosphorus because it has a yellowish tinge—is produced by heating crushed calcium (Ca, element #20) and phosphate rock together with coke—coal that has been heated to drive out the impurities. Coke is mostly pure carbon (C, element #6.)

The production of white phosphorus is generally carried out in a furnace capable of producing very high temperatures. When the materials are heated to 1,500°C (2,700°F), they are converted into phosphorus gas and carbon monoxide (CO) gas. The vapors are collected and cooled to a temperature at which phosphorus turns into a liquid, at which point the carbon monoxide separates off.

The liquid phosphorus collected must be stored underwater to prevent it from reacting with the oxygen in air and bursting into flame. It can be shipped—still in water—in tank cars, or it can be solidified and shipped, also in water, in barrels.

Working with white phosphorus can be hazardous because a compound called phosphine, PH_3, may inadvertently be formed with hydrogen (H, element #1). Phosphine damages the central

Phosphate mining in Florida

nervous system and the liver in humans. In the past, before it was known to be toxic, people working with phosphorus and breathing its fumes sometimes developed a condition that came to be called "phossy jaw." Any mouth wound refused to heal, and eventually the jawbone disintegrated.

The world's largest facility for making elemental phosphorus was located in Newfoundland, Canada. It closed in 1989, but many tons of slag, or rocky waste were left on the site of the plant. The plant location is now a hazardous waste site. Mining of phosphate rock for fertilizer is less hazardous and occurs at many places, including Florida.

Phosphates

As we have seen, elemental white phosphorus exists as a molecule of four atoms arranged like a triangular pyramid. This arrangement is quite unstable and easily changes to something else. In nature, what it does most often is combine with oxygen atoms. Each atom of phosphorus attaches to four atoms of oxygen. This group of atoms is called the phosphate group and is written as PO_4^{3-}. The way it is written indicates that the phosphate group has three more electrons (which are negative, shown by the minus sign) than protons. Actually, PO_4^{3-} is one of the five compounds of phosphorus and oxygen.

Phosphate is a negatively charged group, or anion. It combines with many different positively charged atoms or groups, called cations, to form complex molecules. Phosphate groups tend to remain together no matter what other chemical reactions are going on.

Phosphate compounds are found in rocks, plants, animals, and humans. Compounds are substances made up of two or more elements that are bound together. Carbon makes more compounds than any other element, but phosphorus runs it a close second.

Phosphoric Acid

The main phosphate compound is phosphoric acid, H_3PO_4. An acid is a chemical that easily gives up its hydrogen atoms as ions, H^+. An ion is an atom or a group of atoms that is missing one or more electrons (a positive ion) or has taken up an extra one or more electrons (a negative ion).

Phosphoric acid is frequently prepared by the chemical industry in a two-step process. White phosphorus is burned in the presence of extra oxygen and forms P_4O_{10}. This oxide then reacts with water to form phosphoric acid:

$$P_4 + excess\ O_2 \rightarrow P_4O_{10}$$

$$P_4O_{10} + 6\ H_2O \rightarrow 4H_3PO_4$$

Phosphoric acid is a white solid when it is pure Many manufacturers do not require pure acid. The impure acid they use is a colorless, thick syrup.

This acid is second only to sulfuric acid, H_2SO_4, in the amount manufactured for use in industry. Like sulfuric acid, phosphoric acid is used primarily in the manufacture of fertilizers. It is also one of the major ingredients in cola soft drinks. It adds a slightly fruity flavor.

IN THE EARTH

The elements of Earth are always on the move, but so slowly that this movement cannot really be noticed. Various elements first came to Earth's surface in volcanoes and enriched the soil. Living things take up the elements. When they die, the elements again become part of the soil. Soil sometimes flows into lakes, rivers, and seas, where it settles to the bottom. Over long periods of time, the material, called sediment, that settles, along with shells and bones, hardens into rock. Mountains form, exposing the rock to air and weather, which carry the elements into the soil and sea again.

This is a very simple description of the way some elements cycle through Earth. Sometimes elements become part of substances that don't look at all like other substances that contain the same

Phosphorus and many other elements reach Earth's surface in lava.

elements. But the elements are there just the same.

Phosphorus is the twelfth most abundant element in Earth's crust, but it is the least plentiful of the essential elements that cycle through our environment and our bodies.

The largest amount of phosphorus is in rock, especially under the ocean. Phosphate rock occurs naturally in two forms. About half of it is in igneous deposits. Igneous rocks were formed from slowly cooling magma, the molten rock inside beneath Earth's crust.

Other phosphates are bound up in sedimentary deposits from ancient seas. Long ago, fish bones, fish scales, shells, and seaweeds settled to the bottom and were gradually compressed into rock. Over long centuries, mountains were formed, and these sedimentary deposits were raised above the ocean's surface. The rock, then exposed to air, wind, and water, was broken down into soil, which contains all the elements that were in the rock.

Plants that grow in phosphorus-bearing soil absorb phosphates through their roots. Over time, the plants die or are eaten by animals, which later die. These living things decompose, and the phosphates once again become part of the soil. Phosphorus in the soil can be washed out, or leached, by rainwater and carried into rivers. Eventually, it makes its way back into the ocean, where it is deposited again.

Seawater contains phosphorus. In the upper levels of the ocean, most phosphorus is used up by living things. In the depths, however, there is considerable phosphorus from the decomposition of the living things that settled to the bottom. And that's where, over long periods of time, phosphate rock formed.

Starting with the Rocks

There are several types of phosphate rocks, but the only truly common one is apatite, which is also called calcium phosphate. Apatites are mixtures of minerals, and they exist in several varieties. Some, called fluorapatite, contain fluorine (F, element #9). Chlorapatite contains chlorine. The word *apatite* means "to deceive." It was used for these rocks because the mineral content of the different apatites is so similar.

Fluorapatite is the kind of rock most commonly mined for its phosphates. Apatities are a mixture of minerals.

Deposits of igneous phosphate rocks are located primarily in the Kola Peninsula of Russia, near northern Finland. Huge deposits of igneous phosphate rocks are also found in North Africa. In the United States, the major phosphate rock formations are sedimentary in nature, raised up from ancient seas. They are mined in Montana, Idaho, and Wyoming.

Phosphate rock is often found in conjunction with uranium (U, element #92), so the two minerals are mined together. The element lithium (Li, element #3) is also sometimes found with phosphate rock.

Actually, phosphates are the prime ingredients in more than 200 kinds of minerals. Other phosphate rocks include the brownish-colored monazite, from which the element cerium (Ce, element #58) is mined, as well as vividly colored blue-green turquoise.

In Soil

Phosphorus is among the most abundant nutrients in organic, or once-living, matter in soil. It is second only to nitrogen. If plant and animal matter is dried and separated into its elements, phosphorus is second in weight after nitrogen, making up about 2 percent of the mass. An estimated 363 to 907 kg (800 to 2,000 pounds) of phosphorus are found in each acre (0.4 hectare) of topsoil.

The amount of phosphorus found in soil varies greatly around the world, however. Some soil may contain twenty times more phosphorus than other soils. The highest phosphorus content is in soils derived from phosphate rocks, and where forests or other plants have grown, undisturbed, century after century. Soil in arid areas tends to have more phosphorus than soil in wet areas because there's little rain to wash the element out.

Soil in the northwestern United States has the highest phosphorus content in the nation. The poorest phosphate soil is in the Southeast.

Soil can contain two different kinds of phosphorus—organic and inorganic phosphorus compounds. Inorganic compounds of phosphorus do not contain carbon. For example, phosphate rock is inorganic. Even if it breaks up very finely and mixes with soil, inorganic phosphate is not absorbed by plants because it does not dissolve. Organic compounds are those that contain carbon. They are easily absorbed by a new generation of plants and used again.

Replacing Phosphorus

In nature, without interference by human beings, phosphorus that is absorbed by plants is eventually returned to the soil, from which it is absorbed again. A small amount is lost by erosion of the soil and by rain washing it out.

When land is used for agriculture, however, a large amount of phosphorus is taken away in crops and must then be replaced in the soil. The substances used to replace phosphorus and other elements are called fertilizers because they make the soil fertile, or capable of growing new things. Fields that have been planted over and over without adequate fertilization usually need phosphorus more than any other nutrient.

Phosphates have been used since ancient times to improve the growth of crops. Ancient farmers plowed guano, or dried bird droppings, into their fields. Native Americans put broken bones and fish into the soil when they planted seeds. Of course, these once-living materials contain phosphorus.

When Europeans settled North America, they used manure from their own animals for fertilizer. By the mid-1800s, though, many fields were worn out and producing poor crops. They had

Guano—petrified bird droppings—was once mined for fertilizer as if it were a mineral.

to find a fertilizer that worked better and was easier to handle.

Phosphates were not discovered as compounds until about 1800. The importance of phosphates and their sources became known only gradually. This knowledge sent businessmen to ancient battlefields throughout Europe, where they dug up old skeletons for the phosphorus they contained. The bones were ground up and sold as fertilizer. However, bone itself does not work well. Phosphate binds to the calcium in bones and dissolves only slightly.

Superphosphates

Heinrich Wilhelm Köhler, an Austrian chemist, solved the problem of using bone phosphates in 1831. He dissolved ground-up bone in sulfuric acid, H_2SO_4. The resulting compound was more easily absorbed by plants.

Köhler failed to do anything with his discovery, however, and the manufacture of a useful fertilizer was delayed until 1842. At that time, John B. Lawes received a British patent for the process of treating bone ash with sulfuric acid to make phosphate. He advertised his product as "super phosphate." He also used mineral phosphates in the process, but bone was the prime source for decades.

American farmers didn't pay much attention until James Mapes, a farmer himself as well as the editor of *Working Farmer* magazine, began to advocate treating bone charcoal that had been used in sugar-refining factories with sulfuric acid. In 1852, he began to produce it and sell it.

At the same time, a few people were experimenting with using phosphate rock as a source of phosphorus. Deposits of the rock were found first in England and Spain and then in Canada. Major supplies in the United States were not found until 1867, when a large deposit was located in South Carolina.

At first, the rock was ground fine so that the powder could be directly mixed into soil. That didn't work well because the

Superphosphate fertilizer being applied by airplane to a
mountainside field in New Zealand

phosphate was bound to the calcium in the rock. Then it was
found that the rock, like bone, could be treated with sulfuric
acid, changing its character.

The final product of the chemical reaction is calcium dihydrogen phosphate, $Ca(H_2PO_4)_2$, which contains about 10 percent
phosphorus. It easily dissolves in water and thus can be
absorbed by plant roots.

Unfortunately, in addition to the calcium dihydrogen phosphate, this process also produces calcium sulfate, $CaSO_4$, which
is gypsum or plaster of Paris. The weight of calcium sulfate
caused the fertilizer to weigh more than the original rock. But
chemists found that if they used phosphoric acid, H_3PO_4, instead
of sulfuric acid, this problem was solved. Even better, the use of
phosphoric acid produced a fertilizer that contained more than
twice as much phosphorus as the early method. They called it
triple superphosphate.

A NUTRIENT FOR THE PLANT KINGDOM

Farmers in ancient times knew that their crops grew best when they put bird droppings and bones in the soil as they planted the seeds. They knew, too, that plants grew best in soil that had lots of organic, or once-living, matter. Organic matter in soil that has been decomposed by microorganisms to its natural elements is called humus. Phosphates are important compounds in humus.

In addition to serving as a natural source of nutrients, humus holds moisture in soil. Moisture is important because water actually carries dissolved chemicals from soil into plant roots. When phosphate minerals dissolve, they change to negative ions, or charged molecules, which the roots can absorb.

Children mixing humus with the soil in a vegetable garden to increase its organic matter

As plants die, nature makes new humus. Nature is continuously recycling the elements. Humans have always recycled organic materials too. Farmers who cut their corn and let the stalks decompose in the soil are recycling organic materials.

More recently, this kind of recycling—called composting— has come back into favor as people realized that it has a real advantage over artificial fertilizers. The elements are taken up slowly and do not easily wash away through the soil. It is estimated that up to 20 percent of all phosphorus applied to soil is washed out—leached—by rain before the plants can absorb it. Much of the fertilizer is wasted.

As farmers discovered when they first started using phosphate rock as fertilizer, only water soluble phosphates will be taken up by plants. This probably amounts to less than 10 percent of the phosphorus in the soil at any one time. The remaining 90 percent is insoluble—it does not dissolve in water. However, soluble forms may become insoluble and vice versa, depending on the acidity of the soil.

Humus converts inorganic minerals to soluble ones. The most effective use of superphosphate from mineral sources is to mix it with organic fertilizer, such as from a compost pile.

Fertilizer by the Numbers

German chemist Justus von Liebig demonstrated in the 1860s that plants did not take actual food from the soil and use it to grow, which is what people had long believed. He

Justus von Liebig

Fertilizing spinach with bone meal. This organic fertilizer's N-P-K numbers vary but are often about 5-20-0.

showed that a plant uses chemicals from the soil, water, and air to make new food for itself. He was among the first to use chemical fertilizers.

A student of Liebig's, an American named Samuel William Johnson, became an agricultural chemist at Yale University in Connecticut. He analyzed the compounds in burned plants and separated out nitrogen, phosphates, and potassium oxide, K_2O. He then used these compounds to establish the percentages of these compounds needed by plants. This resulted in the establishment of N-P-K numbers on fertilizers, which actually mean nitrogen (N), phosphates (P), and potassium oxide (K), even though a fertilizer may also contain other compounds.

Not all fertilizers are the same. Farmers or houseplant growers have to choose the right percentages of N-P-K for what they are trying to grow. The package of a typical houseplant fertilizer might say 5-10-5. This means that it contains 5 percent nitrogen, 10 percent phosphorus, and 5 percent potassium (usually called potash). The other 80 percent of the material—a powder or a liquid—is filler that helps to spread the chemicals. The 5-10-5 formula is useful for young plants that are busy growing, and it can be used fairly frequently.

Flowers require more phosphorus to grow than most other plants do, so fertilizers intended for use in flower gardens usually have a higher P number. Lawns, on the other hand, need lots of nitrogen in order to keep producing green grass. Cereal grains, which are grasses, also require a great deal of nitrogen. Vegetables need a balanced formula, with approximately equal amounts of the three elements. A typical formula that is useful for growing tomato plants is 18-18-20.

More recently, fertilizer manufacturers have produced a compound called ammonium monohydrogen phosphate, $(NH_4)_2HPO_4$. This useful compound allows farmers to apply both nitrogen and phosphate at the same time. It has an N-P-K formula of about 18-46-0. Any potassium needed is added in a separate product.

Not all plants require an equal amount of phosphorus. Grain sorghum requires the most, and corn is second. Sugarcane requires the least. All crops use most of the phosphorus they need in the first stages of growth.

Too much phosphorus in plants, especially grasses, may prevent the plant from taking in some of the other nutrients it needs, such as zinc and iron (Fe, element #26). Too little phosphorus makes grass turn red and stop growing.

Plants are very good at indicating when they're not getting enough of an element to thrive. A phosphorus deficiency is revealed by generally poor growth of a young

The stems and the backs of leaves on this corn plant turned red because it did not receive enough phosphorus.

plant and a reddish tinge on the underside of the leaves. A plant with insufficient phosphorus will rarely produce useful seed.

Plants That Help Other Plants

Some plants cannot automatically take what they need from the soil. For example, plant roots cannot take up phosphorus if there is too much aluminum (Al, element #13) in the soil. The situation can be cured by the use of compost. The organic matter in humus forms some organic acids that lock up the aluminum, preventing it from harming the plant roots.

Mycorrhizas are a type of fungi, which are primitive nongreen plants, such as mushrooms. These fungi are sometimes found wrapped around the roots of some higher plants, especially pine trees.

The fungi and the trees need each other. Mycorrhizas help move compounds, such as phosphates, from the soil into the roots. The chemicals accumulate in the tiny threads of the fungus from which it is transferred into the roots. Trees that depend on these chemicals often will not grow adequately if the fungus is not present in the soil. Mycorrhizas are very important in the growth of pine forests.

A slice through a pine-tree rootlet shows a mycorrhiza surrounding it as a ring.

A Hawaiian rain forest was found to have a surprising amount of phosphorus in its soil, unlike the rain forests in South America.

Rain Forests

Plants absorb so much phosphate and other compounds from the soil that they may leave nothing in the soil itself. This is what happens in dense rain forests. In recent years, a great deal of rain forest in Brazil, for example, was cut down, primarily to create farmland for a growing population. However, the soil turned out to be so poor in nutrients that the land was nearly worthless after a year or two. The farmers cannot afford to buy fertilizers to replace the nutrients. As a result, many acres of rain forest were lost for no purpose.

A soil scientist working in Hawaii studied a rain forest on the island of Kauai. The soil in this part of Hawaii has quite inadequate nutrients. It should not be able to support a rain forest, but it does. The scientist found, though, that the phosphorus used by the rain forest blows in across the ocean from a desert in western China, almost 6,500 kilometers (4,000 mi) away.

THE MAGIC MOLECULES

All the processes that take place within a living organism add up to what is called metabolism. Hundreds of different, quite complex processes are involved. They do everything from moving the muscles of a marathon runner to lighting up the tail of a firefly to controlling the complicated photosynthesis of green plants.

Some metabolic processes take food and build molecules from it. These are called *anabolic* processes. Anabolic processes use up energy. Other processes are *catabolic*. They break apart molecules, releasing energy. The basic control of these processes comes from powerful supermolecules in which phosphates play a vital part.

Among the results of the metabolic processes in fireflies is the natural phosphorescence on their lower abdomens.

31

The Basis of Life

DNA—deoxyribonucleic acid—is a complex molecule found in the centers, or nuclei, of cells. DNA makes up genes, the parts of a cell responsible for passing on genetic information from one generation to the next. Genes determine whether a living thing will have long legs, brown hair, veined leaves, or edible seeds. They are responsible for a blue strip in the shell of a clam or the tendency of a woman's body to develop breast cancer.

The DNA in genes establishes a blueprint, or pattern, that gives instructions to another kind of molecule in the nucleus, called RNA, which stands for ribonucleic acid. DNA never leaves the nucleus of the cell. Instead, it gives instructions to RNA, which carries them outside the nucleus. There, the complex molecules called proteins, which make up most of the physical substance of our bodies, are built up. RNA directs the sequences

This computer model shows the intricate and elaborate RNA molecule, which carries instructions from DNA to sites outside the cell's nucleus.

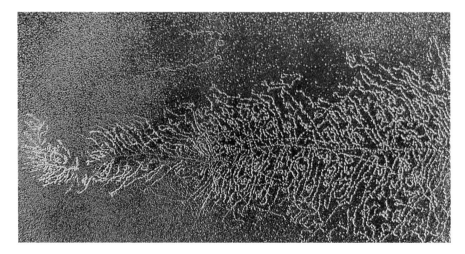

in which the twenty primary amino acids form the building blocks of proteins. These proteins will result in the characteristics determined by the genes.

The most important function of proteins is to serve as enzymes. These chemicals act as catalysts, speeding up reactions but not taking part in them. There are hundreds of enzymes in our bodies, each one doing a very specific job. Enzymes are so specific that an enzyme and the chemical it works on fit together like a lock and key. No other enzyme key fits the lock of a specific chemical.

Supermolecules

Both DNA and RNA are supermolecules. They are made up of chains of repeating subunits, or smaller molecules, called nucleotides. Each nucleotide has three parts: one type of molecule called a base, another that is a type of sugar, and a phosphate molecule. The phosphate holds the other two parts together.

The different functions of DNA and RNA are the result of two seemingly small differences in their structures. First, in the sugar part of the nucleotide, RNA's sugar molecule is a type called ribose. DNA's sugar molecule has one fewer atom of oxygen and is called *deoxy*ribose. Second, the bases in RNA are four molecules called adenine, guanine, cytosine, and uracil. Three of the bases in DNA are the same, but the uracil is replaced by thymine.

The four repeating bases in DNA can be arranged in an infinite, or endless, number of ways. This fact accounts for the seemingly infinite number of genetic characteristics in humans. The long chains of DNA determine the genetic code that controls heredity. Long chains of genes—about 10,000—make a unit called a chromosome. There are 23 pairs of chromosomes in each human cell.

The chromosomes duplicate themselves in a process called meiosis. In a female, half the contents of the chromosomes go into one egg and half into another. A male's chromosomes split among the sperm. When a male sperm and a female egg join in sexual reproduction, the two incomplete sets of chromosomes link up, providing the genetic information for a whole person.

A few years ago, it was said that each chromosome has an infinite number of genes that control everything about a person—sex, hair color, eye color, likely weight, intelligence, genetic diseases, aging characteristics, and so on. Recently, though, scientists have been analyzing each gene in the total genetic make-up of humans, called the human genome. For example, scientists can now locate the gene that controls a specific genetic disease. They hope in the future to be able to fix such genes so that an individual will not develop a debilitating disease. More than 3,000 identified diseases involve genes to some extent.

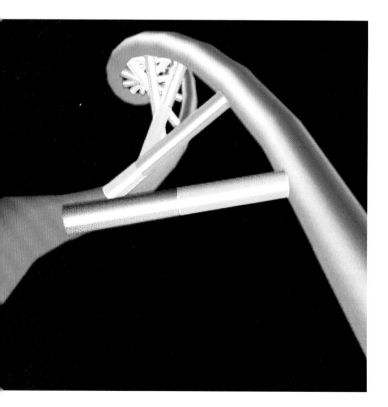

In this model of a tiny portion of a DNA molecule, each color on a crossbar represents one of the four repeating bases. They are held together by a phosphate.

Calories and Oxygen

You've probably heard of calories. A calorie is a unit of measurement of heat energy in food. Energy is used to hold the chemicals in food together. Food is broken down considerably before it can be used by the body. The pizza that you eat doesn't do a cell within your body any good, but the sugar that is derived from the flour and the tomato sauce being broken apart into different molecules can be burned, or oxidized, in a cell for energy.

We tend to think of respiration as something that occurs in our lungs—they take in air, pass the oxygen content of the air into the bloodstream and take back carbon dioxide, CO_2, from the blood and exhale it.

But in reality, respiration happens at the cellular level. Oxygen enters each cell, reacts with—oxidizes—some of the organic (carbon-containing) compounds that originated in the food we ate, and leaves the cells as carbon dioxide. Heat energy is given off in the process.

$$C + O_2 \rightarrow CO_2 + \text{heat energy}$$

carbon + oxygen $\rightarrow$ carbon dioxide + heat energy

During digestion, the molecules from food are broken down into simpler molecules. Carbohydrates (the pizza crust) become simple sugars, or glucose. Proteins (the sausage or pepperoni) break down into amino acids. Fats (cheese) remain fats.

Much of the energy used to keep an organism functioning comes from its current food supply—the pizza. Inside cells, these simple molecules are oxidized, or burned, giving off heat, which keeps us warm and alive.

The remainder of the energy needed for life—almost 70 percent—is stored for use as needed. That's where the magic phosphorus-containing molecule comes in.

ATP for Energy

Whether plant or animal, cells of living organisms store energy in a chemical called adenosine triphosphate, ATP. Its function in an organism's cells is to take some of the current food and hold the energy in it for later use. ATP has been likened to a flashlight battery, storing energy for when it is needed.

When is it needed? ATP provides energy for muscles to move. It also plays a role in the manufacture of proteins, the transmission of messages along nerve cells, and the production of chemicals by glands.

ATP is a complex chemical with a tail made up of three phosphate groups, HPO_4^{2-}. In a phosphate group, the phosphorus atom and each oxygen atom actually share electrons so that each atom has a stable outer, or valence, electron shell.

Energy is stored in the bond that holds the phosphates together. The phosphate bond is called a high-energy bond. If the bond is broken, energy is released.

When messengers in the cell indicate that energy is needed, the phosphate group at the end of the "tail" of an ATP molecule breaks away, releasing heat energy. The result is ADP (adenosine *di*phosphate, because there are now only two phosphate groups instead of three) plus the first phosphate. That phosphate is now an ion, with an electric charge, because the electron shells are no longer balanced.

No living thing can keep changing its ATP into ADP. There has to be a way to make new ATP. This happens in a complex building-up, or anabolic, process, in which an enzyme attaches the loose phosphate ion to an ADP molecule. This process is called oxidative phosphorylation. The energy for it comes from the burning, or oxidation, of glucose.

In both animals and plants, ATP is produced in cells inside tiny shoe-shaped bodies called mitochondria. A mitochondrion

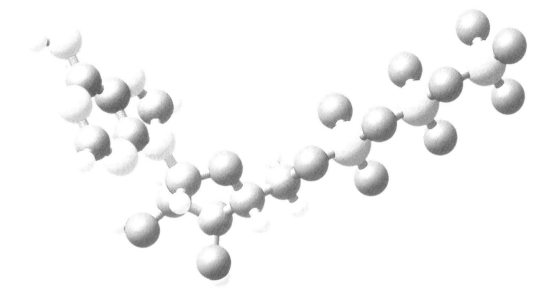

An ATP molecule (shown in a computer model). The three phosphates at the right are attached to the adenosine. Energy is available in the cell when the bond between the second and third phosphate is broken.

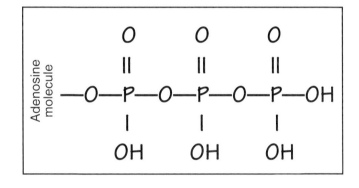

contains many folded surfaces that provide a huge amount of space along which oxidation takes place.

It is in oxidative phosphorylation that the oxygen you breathe is used. The oxygen atoms, O_2, are converted to water, and the energy from that process is used to convert ADP to ATP. If a person dies from lack of oxygen, it is actually the conversion process that is failing.

PHOSPHORUS FOR PEOPLE

Aerobic exercise—outdoors or indoors—strengthens bones and muscles and increases the oxygen use of the body.

Some elements play a role in the physical structure of the body. Others contribute to the chemical function of metabolism. Phosphorus in the animal body does both.

The food we eat, especially high-protein foods such as red meats and milk products, contain a great deal of phosphorus. In fact, everything we eat has phosphorus in it because the element is present in every cell of every living thing.

Phosphorus also plays a role in the energy made in each cell, the energy needed to carry on life. This happens because the simple sugar, or glucose, that is the end product of digestion is stored as a more complex substance called glycogen. When glucose is needed by the body, glycogen is broken back down by enzymes, some of which contain phosphates.

Blood and Bone

When food reaches the intestine, the phosphorus content is separated out by enzymes called phosphatases (the "ase" ending on a compound name means that it's an enzyme). It enters the bloodstream in the form of different negative phosphate ions. In blood plasma—the thin fluid in which blood cells move—the ions help keep the blood from getting too acid or too basic. They carry out this function by attaching themselves to, or letting go of, hydrogen ions, which are positive, when the acid-base balance needs adjusting.

If the blood is too acid—has too many hydrogen ions—this is the reaction:

$$HPO_4{}^{2-} + H^+ \rightarrow H_2PO^{4-}$$

The phosphate ions neutralize the excess hydrogen ions, returning the blood to its normal acid-base state.

Or, if the blood has become too basic (with too few hydrogen ions and too many hydroxyl, OH^-, ions), the reaction works like this:

$$H_2PO + OH^- \rightarrow HPO_4{}^{2-} + H_2O$$

The phosphate content of blood is tied to the phosphate content of bone because bone serves as a "storage cabinet" for phosphate. The content of phosphate in blood is controlled by parathormone, the hormone given off by the parathyroid glands. These glands are located in the neck, on the larger thyroid glands. Parathormone works through vitamin D.

If there isn't enough phosphate in the blood, the parathormone removes phosphate molecules from bone. If there's too

Normal bone tissue, on the left, is considerably more solid than the tissue on the right, which came from a person with osteoporosis—a thinning of the bones caused by a lack of calcium and phosphorus.

much phosphate in the blood, the spare molecules are deposited in bone. The body doesn't properly absorb phosphorus from food if there is not enough vitamin D present.

We think of bone as a solid, unchanging framework for our bodies. But actually, bone is dynamic. It continually takes in and releases the ions from which it is made. These are calcium ions, Ca^{2+}, and phosphate ions, PO_4^{3-}. About 10 percent of the elements in bone are being transformed at any one time, and yet bones always seem solid.

The making of bone is often referred to as calcification. It is more properly called mineralization, because phosphorus is just as important as calcium. The primary mineral of bone is any of several different calcium phosphates, or apatites. The most common is hydroxyapatite, $Ca_{10}(PO_4)_6(OH)_2$.

Hydroxyapatite also makes up the hard outer surface of teeth (the inside is soft). However, it's not so hard that it can't be eroded by the chemicals in plaque, the sugary material that forms on teeth. Plaque can contain bacteria that eat away the hard material, making cavities that must be repaired. Plaque needs to be brushed away as often as possible.

Phosphate, as well as calcium, is normally present in saliva. If plaque is removed from the mouth by regular brushing, the ions in saliva are sufficient to keep the minerals in the hydroxyapatite replaced.

Ions at Work

About 90 percent of the phosphorus in the body is found in the bones and teeth, and yet that other 10 percent is what keeps the body functioning, especially at the cellular level. Phosphate ions are found in the fluids of the body, both outside and inside cells, but primarily inside. They do several jobs in the body in addition to making up part of ATP and nucleic acids.

The plaque on teeth (visible here as the brown spots in crevices) must be removed if the phosphate in saliva is going to do its work in the mouth.

Ions in blood, in other body fluids, and inside cells are called electrolytes because they have an electrical charge. Positive electrolytes, called cations, are positive because their atoms have one, two, or even three fewer electrons than they have protons in the atomic nucleus. Sodium (Na^+) and potassium (K^+) are the main positive electrolytes. (Sodium is Na, element #11.) Negative electrolytes, called anions, have more electrons than they have protons. In addition to phosphate, PO_4^{3-}, chloride (Cl^-) is the main negative electrolyte.

One of the tasks of phosphate ions in cells is to transport

other nutrients through the cell membranes. They do this by combining with the other substances in a process called phosphorylation. The phosphate ions serve as an "on-off switch" for these nutrients, especially in the manufacture of proteins.

For example, phosphate molecules control the transport of calcium through the body cells. Calcium ions, Ca^{2+}, have a tendency to react with phosphate ions, PO_4^{3-}, forming a solid substance. Such a substance would clog up the cells of the body, so the two kinds of ions must be kept apart.

The cells solve the problem by keeping calcium ions outside the cell and the phosphate ions inside the cell except when needed. Then special one-way channels open in the cell membrane, allowing calcium ions inside.

Calcium channels are used by cells of the nervous system. They are also important to the heart. Calcium ions help the heart muscle contract. If the heart is diseased and needs to beat less often so that it can rest, a physician may prescribe a medicine called a calcium channel blocker.

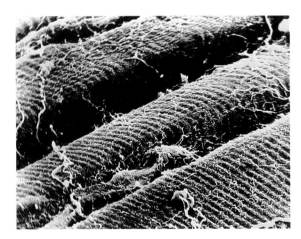

A close-up of human muscle fiber (with color added) called striated muscle. Such muscles are under the voluntary control of the person. They get their first burst of energy from ATP.

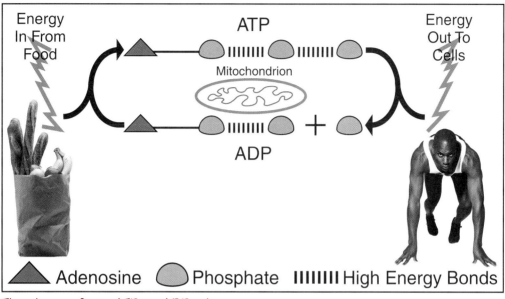

Energy In From Food   **ATP**   **Energy Out To Cells**

Mitochondrion

ADP

▲ Adenosine   ⬭ Phosphate   ‖‖‖‖‖‖ High Energy Bonds

The change from ATP to ADP releases energy.

Muscles and ATP

In all living organisms, ATP is continually being built and utilized for the energy to carry on the activities of the cells. In animals, though, it has a critical third role—it controls the action of the muscles.

ATP is stored until it is needed. In muscle cells it's needed to make muscle fibers contract. Muscle fiber is made up of two separate long, thin strands of proteins, actin and myosin. When ATP is released by the surrounding cells, it makes the two proteins move closer together, thus contracting the muscle.

However, only a small amount of ATP is stored and ready. After the initial burst of energy from this phosphorus-containing chemical storehouse, other compounds take over to keep muscles moving. Once the muscles relax, though, the ADP will have a chance to change back into ATP and build up again.

Some forms of exercise, such as walking or running, get the ATP continuously recycling because a continuous supply of energy is provided. However, in exercise requiring a burst of energy, such as lifting weights, the energy supply is quickly used up and can't be replaced until the body gets a chance to rest.

Holding It All Together

The phosphorus in bone is an inorganic mineral. But the same phosphorus compounds in substances called phospholipids are organic, or carbon-containing, compounds. *Lipid* is the general name for all fats and oils. These substances all have difficulty dissolving in water. Phospholipids are important because they can make lipids and water work together.

Some phospholipids are ingredients in cell membranes. These membranes are not just the wrapping that holds the cell's contents together. They also control what substances are let into and out of the cell. These membranes truly control metabolism.

One of the most significant phospholipids is lecithin. It is a major component of cell membranes that lets some chemicals through but not others. Some people who are interested in mineral supplements have claimed that extra doses of lecithin can benefit the heart and slow the onset of the terrible brain condition called Alzheimer's disease. There is no real proof of these claims, however. Some people take lecithin supplements in the hope that it will slow the aging process. Others expect it to help them lose weight. Again, there's no proof of these claims.

A group of medications called bisphosphonates are being studied as possible aids against osteoporosis, or thinning of the bone, as in the photo on page 40. This condition occurs in millions of women as they get older. Thin bone becomes brittle and breaks easily. The bisphosphonates imitate the action of estrogens, a group of hormones that are produced by a woman's body until menopause. Osteoporosis usually does not occur in women until after their regular menstrual cycles have stopped. Bisphosphonates are also being tested for their usefulness in preventing bone damage from cancer.

Too Much of a Good Thing

It is recommended that people get equal amounts of phosphorus and calcium for both to be used properly. However, most Americans don't get enough calcium. In addition, their bodies may not

Farms are the source of much of the phosphorus and calcium our bodies need. Cattle provide both red meat and milk.

absorb what calcium they do get because it has to compete with excess phosphorus to be absorbed. People who drink a lot of cola soft drinks—which may contain as much as 500 milligrams of phosphorus in one can—get far too much of the element. It is excreted by the kidneys in urine.

Too much phosphorus can contribute to dental decay because it pulls calcium out of the teeth. It may also play a role in heart disease.

As we discussed earlier, phosphates help maintain the acid-base balance in blood. While in the blood, though, they do something else—they help the body use the nutrient iron, which is one of the trace elements that are necessary only in small amounts for human life.

Some iron is quickly bound up in the complex molecule

called heme. This molecule carries oxygen in a substance called hemoglobin in red blood cells. But more than 30 percent of iron is not used this way—it's *nonheme* iron. Nonheme iron is used in such activities as building bone and cartilage during growth, and in keeping the health-maintaining immune system strong. Too much phosphorus or calcium can prevent this iron from being absorbed.

It's recommended that people get between 800 and 1,500 milligrams of phosphorus every day—about four 8-ounce (0.2-l) glasses of milk. This would also give an individuals the daily requirement of calcium they need if they are not lactose intolerant (allergic to some of the chemicals in milk). However, unless people are actually starving, they are unlikely to suffer severe phosphorus deficiency.

It is possible, though, to have just a little less phosphorus than the body requires. This condition happens primarily with people who take a lot of antacids to ease stomach discomfort. The magnesium (Mg, element #12) or aluminum in antacids can prevent the body from utilizing the phosphorus that it does get. This situation may also happen in people who drink too much alcohol.

Someone who doesn't get enough vitamin D might not absorb all the phosphorus they need in their intestines. Vitamin D is needed for both phosphorus and calcium to be absorbed. Diarrhea, a symptom of many different medical conditions, can reduce the amount of phosphorus in the blood.

Of course, the continual supply of phosphorus we take in with food does not build up in the body. If it did, our bones would continue to grow and our teeth might become the size of rocks. Phosphorus not being used by the bones, teeth, and cells is collected in the kidneys and excreted in urine—which explains why alchemist Hennig Brand was able to discover the element in urine.

AWASH IN PHOSPHORUS

Water that contains a lot of minerals, especially calcium and magnesium ions, is called "hard" water. For centuries, people who washed clothing with soap in hard water could do nothing about the yucky gray scum that formed on the water and lingered on the clothing. The scum was the product of the positive calcium and magnesium ions in water reacting with negative ions in the soap ingredients.

In the 1930s, soap substitutes called synthetic detergents were developed. After World War II, automatic washing machines became popular. So did these detergents. The major ingredient in synthetic detergents is one or more forms of sodium phosphate.

Sodium phosphate comes in a variety of molecules. These molecules differ in the number of atoms of sodium, hydro-

The same farms that supply milk and meat containing phosphorus may pollute nearby rivers with excess phosphorus in fertilizers.

gen, phosphorus, and oxygen they contain, but they are all called sodium phosphate. They are all made from the reaction of phosphoric acid, H_3PO_4, with sodium carbonate, Na_2CO_3. The resulting molecules can be MSP, which is monosodium phosphate (NaH_2PO_4), or DSP, which is disodium phosphate (Na_2HPO_4). Or they might be more complex varieties such as TSP (trisodium phosphate) or STPP (sodium tripolyphosphate).

They all have different uses, though most are used in cleaning. Today, TSP is used as an important cleaner used in poultry-processing plants to wash away harmful bacteria, especially those that cause the disease salmonella.

STPP was the main ingredient in detergents until the 1980s, when manufacturers voluntarily reduced the amount of phosphorus. In laundry detergents, it isolates calcium, thus making the water softer. It also kept the dirt from returning to the clothing being washed. Dishwashing detergents still use a lot of STPP.

Killing Lakes and Rivers

While Americans were enjoying how easy synthetic detergents made it for them to do their laundry, something bad was happening to rivers and lakes. By the 1960s and 1970s, people who lived in the country began to notice that some lakes and rivers were beginning to look pretty strange. The water was getting cloudy. Sometimes there was foam on the surface. Bad smells came out of the mud along the edges and from the bottom. The lakes were no longer good places for fish and other animals to live.

What was happening was a process called eutrophication. A eutrophic lake is one that's filled with nutrients. That sounds like a good thing, until you realize that a eutrophic lake is getting *too* full of nutrients, especially phosphorus.

With lots of nutrients, the primitive plants called algae—which you sometimes see as green scum on ponds—were

Too much algae in a body of water may result from excess phosphorus in runoff from farms.

growing like mad. In the normal cycle of nature, dead plants are decomposed by bacteria. However, with so many plants to be decomposed, the number of bacteria increased in the phosphate-laced water. They used up all the oxygen, leaving none for fish and other water life. Except for algae, living things disappeared. The body of water became "dead."

It looked as if the culprit in killing these bodies of water was the phosphate in detergents. Finally, about 1990, public officials began to accept that there was a problem. Most states and many cities banned the use of phosphate-containing detergent.

Detergents were certainly not alone in being the bad guys. Many farmers spread manure on their fields to take care of their fertilizer needs. However, if enough of this animal waste is spread into the soil to meet the need for nitrogen, the fields get too much phosphorus. The phosphates that the crops can't take up may be carried by rainwater into nearby lakes and rivers.

To make matters worse, there is an old belief among some farmers that phosphates in the diet of their livestock can improve reproduction. But in reality, all the extra phosphorus does is go through the animals and out with their waste.

Phosphates from Sewage

The average adult human eliminates about 1.5 grams (1/2 ounce) of phosphorus from his or her body every day. This translates into a lot of phosphorus going through the sewage- treatment system. Detergents, even toothpaste, also contribute to the phosphorus load.

The main task of sewage treatment is to remove harmful bacteria and bad-smelling chemicals before the water is returned to rivers and lakes. The solid matter left after water is removed from sewage is called sludge. Sewage sludge contains about 4 percent phosphorus.

Sweden recognized that phosphorus and some other minerals needed by plants make their way from farms to urban areas because most of the people who eat the crops live in cities. That nation is working to return phosphorus to rural areas by using dried sludge as fertilizer in farm fields. About 30 percent of Sweden's fertilizer comes from sewage-treatment plants.

Searching for Answers

As with most large problems, many different parts of society need to become involved in solving the problem of too much phosphorus in the environment. Farmers need to use less chemical fertilizer. Sewage-treatment plants need to deal with more of the minerals being lost in sewage treatment. People need to change their attitude toward sludge as a source of fertilizer.

Perhaps the way we raise farm animals needs to be changed so that less phosphorus gets into manure. Since phosphorus is a natural nutrient in cattle and pig feed, perhaps we can find a way to provide nutrients without providing an excess that ends up in manure. Pig farms are a major cause of phosphorus pollution. Canadian scientists are trying to breed pigs that produce manure with less phosphorus.

Perhaps changing the crops would help. In the late 1990s, an agricultural scientist developed a species of giant soybeans that take 75 percent more phosphorus from the soil than regular soybeans do. The plan is to grow them in places where excess phosphorus in the soil threatens nearby waterways. The Eastern Shore of Maryland, on the ocean and Chesapeake Bay, is one such location where this will be tried.

A
PHOSPHORUS
CATALOG

On the Moon

When you look at a full moon, you can sometimes see large areas that look like dark shadows on the white disk. These are large, flat regions that were once thought to be seas. They were called *maria,* which is the plural of *mare,* from the Latin word for "sea." When the Apollo 15 flight landed at Mare Imbrium (the "Sea of Rains") in 1971, it was discovered that the rock making up the flat surface was the last remains of the age of great lava flows in the moon's history.

The rock is an unusual substance that the scientists call KREEP, short for *K* (the symbol of potassium), *R*are-*E*arth *E*lements, and *P*hosphorus. "Rare earth" is the name given long ago to the elements

Apollo 15 astronauts explore the lunar surface at Mare Imbrium.

in Group 3 in the Periodic Table of the Elements. They include scandium (Sc, element #21), yttrium (Y, #39), and the lanthanide series (#57 through #71).

Poisons

Several chemical-warfare weapons belong to a category of chemicals called the organic phosphorus, or organophosphorus, group. They contain phosphorus atoms bonded directly to carbon atoms. The similar-sounding organophosphates, which are used in less lethal insecticides, do not have that feature.

One organophosphorus compound is sarin, a nerve gas that paralyzes the central nervous system. One of its prime ingredients is methyl-phosphonic dichloride. The Germans, who discovered it in 1937, developed it during World War II. It's been said that they had enough stockpiled by the end of the war to kill every human on the planet. Fortunately, it was never used.

The Cloud Marks the Spot

When white phosphorus combusts (oxidizes), a lingering white cloud of phosphorus pentoxide, P_2O_5, hangs over the site of the combustion. The military has long used such clouds to conceal troops. This can't be done too often, however, because the fumes in the cloud are toxic. Sometimes, the chemical is shot out of artillery at a target. The cloud that forms marks the target for other gunners.

Takeover by Termites

The Cretaceous Period of Earth's history began about 144 million years ago, with our planet's land masses populated by large, heavy dinosaurs. But over time, dinosaurs became progressively smaller, and many lost their heavy bony armor. Several species even lost their teeth.

Some scientists in Australia, where the change was particularly noticeable, think that the amount of available phosphorus in the environment was shrinking. This may have been caused by the vast growth in the numbers of termites, which take a lot of phosphorus from the soil and utilize it in the paths they follow and in their mounds. Even today, the soil in areas of the world where termites abound—primarily tropical areas—are deficient in phosphorus.

Antlers Too Large

The Irish elk is a deer that lived in western Europe until about 15,000 years ago. It developed antlers so huge that they caused the animals a great deal of trouble. Their antlers sometimes spread 3 meters (10 ft) across. The antlers could get caught among trees, trapping the animal and causing it to starve to death.

Paleontologists (scientists who study ancient life through fossil remains) have discovered that these animals' bodies lost phosphorus from their bones during the antler-growing season in spring and summer. Then the phosphorus returned to their bones during the winter after the antlers had been shed. The weakening of their bones may have been one reason the Irish elk died out.

Rough turquoise

Phosphate Gems

The semiprecious blue-green stone called turquoise is a phosphate rock that also contains copper and aluminum. (Copper is Cu, element #29.) The color comes from the copper. Originally found in the Middle East, turquoise reached Europe through Turkey. *Turquoise* is a

French word meaning "Turkish."

A darker blue crystal called lazurite (which comes from the Latin *lazur,* meaning "blue") is also a phosphate mineral used in jewelry. It contains magnesium and iron instead of copper.

Exercise Confusion

Some exercise specialists think that taking extra phosphates may help endurance runners and other athletes maintain peak performance in a race. Apparently, one study showed that taking a sodium phosphate supplement lowered the levels of lactic acid in the muscles, which allowed them to work longer. Lactic acid is the compound that makes muscles hurt after too much exercise. Other studies found that sodium phosphate might produce a boost in a short-term high-intensity burst of activity, such as a sprint, but has no effect in an endurance activity, such as running a marathon.

Holding Back the Fires

As long ago as the early 1800s, theater curtains were soaked in liquid ammonium phosphate to make them less flammable. Today, this chemical is still used on some fabrics, though only those meant to be dry-cleaned. They can withstand the other chemicals used in dry-cleaning, but not the water used in laundering.

Phosphorus-based chemicals are the main flame retardants used on clothing, especially children's clothing, that are made from cotton. They work best on the cellulose fiber in materials that originally came from plants, such as cotton and linen. However, some phosphorus-based flame retardants can be incorporated in the actual compounds used in making synthetic fibers such as polyester.

Materials used in electronic equipment are usually made of plastics that contain halogens—those elements in Group 17 . But halogens are corrosive; they eat away the things they touch.

Creating Radioactive Isotopes

In 1934, Irène and Jean Frédéric Joliot-Curie made the first artificial radioactive isotope. They bombarded atoms of the element aluminum with alpha particles and turned it into an isotope of phosphorus.

An alpha particle is the nucleus of a helium (He, element #2) atom. It has just two protons and two neutrons. When alpha particles strike the nuclei of aluminum atoms, some of the protons from the helium become part of those nuclei, changing the aluminum, which has 13 protons, into phosphorus, which has 15 protons. But this new phosphorus gave off radiation, which meant it was still breaking down. It was radioactive!

The Joliot-Curies received the 1935 Nobel Prize in chemistry for their development of the first artificial radioactive isotope. Today, there are hundreds of isotopes, which are used for many different purposes in both medicine and industry.

When an alpha particle crashes into the nucleus of an aluminum atom, it adds two protons to the nucleus, changing it into a radioactive phosphorus isotope.

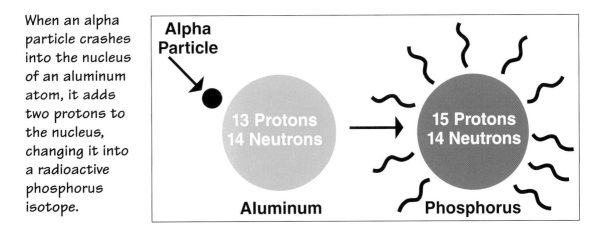

The Revealing Radioisotope

Phosphorus-32 is an isotope that has 17 neutrons in the nucleus instead of the usual 16. It is made artificially by bombarding phosphorus atoms with neutrons. The resulting radioactive isotope gives off high-energy gamma rays that can be identified on special machines.

Phosphorus-32 is one of several radioisotopes that are useful in medical diagnosis because it goes harmlessly through the body when injected into the bloodstream. It tends to accumulate at the site of tumors, especially in the eye and the brain. A special scanning machine can pinpoint where the radioisotope has accumulated, making a picture of the area where the surgeon can safely operate to remove the tumor.

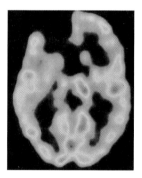

Brain scans made after radioactive phosphorus has been injected into the body reveals a brain with a tumor (left), compared to a normal brain (right).

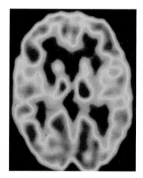

Working in Silicon Valley

The element silicon (Si, element #14) has given its name to a number of places where many high-tech electronics companies are clustered, especially the original "Silicon Valley" located near San Francisco. Silicon itself is not a very good conductor of electricity, which seems odd for a material known as a *semi*conductor. Other elements must be added to improve silicon's ability to

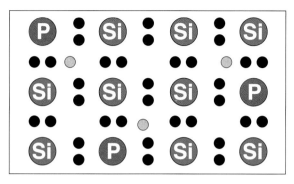

When silicon atoms (blue) share electrons with phosphorus atoms (pink), one electron is left over (gray) and is free to carry an electric current.

work in printed circuits or tiny computer chips.

Phosphorus is one of those elements. Phosphorus is right next to silicon on the Periodic Table. It has one more electron (and, of course, one more proton) than silicon, so, as part of a silicon compound, it has an electron to spare. This free electron can move around the material and, with other free electrons, set up an electric current through the silicon. With careful arrangement of such extra atoms, a complex electrical circuit can be created in a very tiny space.

A computer chip magnified 180 times shows the electrical circuits as narrow grooves. At the atomic level, the electrical circuits are creating by mixing phosphorus, or other elements, with silicon.

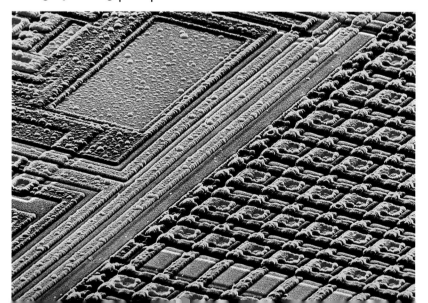

Phosphorus in Brief

Name: phosphorus, from the Greek word meaning "bearer of light"
Symbol: P
Discovered by: Hennig Brand in 1669
Atomic number: 15
Atomic weight: 30.9738
Electrons in shells: 2, 8, 5
Group: 15; other elements in Group 15 include nitrogen, arsenic, antimony, and bismuth
Usual characteristics of most common allotrope: white waxy non-metal
Density (mass per unit volume) of white P: 1.82 g/cm³
Melting point (freezing point) of white P: 44.1°C (111.4°F)
Boiling point (liquefaction point) of white P: 280°C (536°F)
Abundance:
    Universe: about 7,000 parts per billion
    Earth: 12th most abundant
    Earth's crust: 12th most abundant element at 3.4%
    Earth's atmosphere: None
    Human body: 6th most abundant element, making up about 1% of the body by weight
Stable isotopes: only P-31
Radioactive isotopes: P-29, P-30, P-32, P-33, P34

Glossary

acid: definitions vary, but basically it is a corrosive substance that gives up a positive hydrogen ion (H+), equal to a proton when dissolved in water; indicates less than 7 on the pH scale because of its large number of hydrogen ions

alkali: a substance, such as an hydroxide or carbonate of an alkali metal, that when dissolved in water causes an increase in the hydroxide ion (OH-) concentration, forming a basic solution.

allotrope: an alternative structure of an element when it exists in two or more forms.

amino acid: one of the building blocks of protein. Twenty are essential for humans.

anion: an ion with a negative charge

atom: the smallest amount of an element that exhibits the properties of the element, consisting of protons, electrons, and (usually) neutrons

base: a substance that accepts a hydrogen ion (H+) when dissolved in water; indicates higher than 7 on the pH scale because of its small number of hydrogen ions

boiling point: the temperature at which a liquid at normal pressure evaporates into a gas, or a solid changes directly (sublimes) into a gas

bond: the attractive force linking atoms together in a molecule or crystal

catalyst: a substance that causes or speeds a chemical reaction without itself being consumed in the reaction

cation: an ion with a positive charge

chemical reaction: a transformation or change in a substance involving the electrons of the chemical elements making up the substance

compound: a substance formed by two or more chemical elements bound together by chemical means

covalent bond: a link between two atoms made by the atoms sharing electrons

decompose: to break down a substance into its components

density: the amount of material in a given volume, or space; mass per unit volume; often stated as grams per cubic centimeter (g/cm³)

dissolve: to spread evenly throughout the volume of another substance

DNA: deoxyribonucleic acid, a chemical in the nucleus of each living cell, which carries genetic information

double bond: the sharing of two pairs of electrons between two atoms in a molecule

electrolyte: a substance that when dissolved in water or when liquefied conducts electricity

element: a substance that cannot be split chemically into simpler substances that maintain the same characteristics. Each of the 103 naturally occurring chemical elements is made up of atoms of the same kind.

evaporate: to change from a liquid to a gas

gas: a state of matter in which the atoms or molecules move freely, matching the shape and volume of the container holding it

group: a vertical column in the Periodic Table, with each element having similar physical and chemical characteristics; also called chemical family

half-life: the period of time required for half of a radioactive element to decay

hormone: any of various secretions of the endocrine glands that control different functions of the body, especially at the cellular level

inorganic: not containing carbon

ion: an atom or molecule that has acquired an electric charge by gaining or losing one or more electrons

ionic bond: a link between two atoms made by one atom taking one or more electrons from the other, giving the two atoms opposite electrical charges, which holds them together

isotope: an atom with a different number of neutrons in its nucleus from other atoms of the same element

mass number: the total of protons and neutrons in the nucleus of an atom

melting point: the temperature at which a solid becomes a liquid

metal: a chemical element that conducts electricity, usually shines, or reflects light, is dense, and can be shaped. About three-quarters of the naturally occurring elements are metals. (Not all metals are elements.)

metalloid: a chemical element that has some characteristics of a metal and some of a nonmetal; includes some elements in Groups 13 through 17 in the Periodic Table

molecule: the smallest amount of a substance that has the characteristics of the substance and usually consists of two or more atoms

neutral: 1) having neither acidic nor basic properties; 2) having no electrical charge

neutron: a subatomic particle within the nucleus of all atoms except hydrogen; has no electric charge

nonmetal: a chemical element that does not conduct electricity, is not dense, and is too brittle to be worked. Nonmetals easily form ions, and they include some elements in Groups 14 through 17 and all of Group 18 in the Periodic Table.

nucleus: 1) the central part of an atom, which has a positive electrical charge from its one or more protons; the nuclei of all atoms except hydrogen also include electrically neutral neutrons; 2) the central portion of most living cells, which controls the activities of the cells and contains the genetic material

organic: containing carbon

oxidation: the loss of electrons during a chemical reaction; need not necessarily involve the element oxygen

pH: a measure of the acidity of a substance, on a scale of 0 to 14, with 7 being neutral. pH stands for "potential of hydrogen."

photosynthesis: in green plants, the process by which carbon dioxide and water, in the presence of light, are turned into sugars

pressure: the force exerted by an object divided by the area over which the force is exerted. The air at sea level exerts a pressure, called atmospheric pressure, of 14.7 pounds per square inch (1013 millibars).

protein: a complex biological chemical made by the linking of many amino acids

proton: a subatomic particle within the nucleus of all atoms; has a positive electric charge

radical: an atom or molecule that contains an unpaired electron

radioactive: of an atom, spontaneously emitting high-energy particles

reduction: the gain of electrons, which occurs in conjunction with oxidation

respiration: the process of taking in oxygen and giving off carbon dioxide

salt: any compound that, with water, results from the neutralization of an acid by a base. In common usage, sodium chloride (table salt)

shell: a region surrounding the nucleus of an atom in which one or more electrons can occur. The inner shell can hold a maximum of two electrons; others may hold eight or more. If an atom's outer, or valence, shell does not hold its maximum number of electrons, the atom is subject to chemical reactions.

solid: a state of matter in which the shape of the collection of atoms or molecules does not depend on the container

solution: a mixture in which one substance is evenly distributed throughout another

sublime: to change directly from a solid to a gas without becoming a liquid first

ultraviolet: electromagnetic radiation which has a wavelength shorter than visible light

valence electron: an electron located in the outer shell of an atom, available to participate in chemical reactions

vitamin: any of several organic substances, usually obtainable from a balanced diet, that the human body needs for specific physiological processes to take place

For Further Information

BOOKS

Atkins, P. W. *The Periodic Kingdom: A Journey into the Land of the Chemical Elements.* NY: Basic Books, 1995

Emsley, John. *Molecules at an Exhibition: Portraits of intriguing materials in everyday life.* Oxford: Oxford U Press, 1998

Heiserman, David L. *Exploring Chemical Elements and Their Compounds,* Blue Ridge Summit, PA: Tab Books, 1992

Hoffman, Roald, and Vivian Torrence. *Chemistry Imagined: Reflections on Science.* Washington, DC: Smithsonian Institution Press, 1993

Newton, David E. *Chemical Elements: From Carbon to Krypton.* 3 volumes. Detroit: UXL, 1998

CD-ROM

Discover the Elements: The Interactive Periodic Table of the Chemical Elements, Paradigm Interactive, Greensboro, NC, 1995

INTERNET SITES

Note that useful sites on the Internet can change and even disappear. If the following site addresses do not work, use a search engine that you find useful, such as:
Yahoo:

> http://www.yahoo.com

or Google:

> http://google.com

A very thorough listing of the major characteristics, uses, and compounds of all the chemical elements can be found at a site called WebElements:

> http://www.shef.ac.uk/~chem/we b-elements/

A Canadian site on the Nature of the Environment includes a large section on the elements in the various Earth systems:

> http://www.cent.org/geo12/geo12/htm

Colored photos of various molecules, cells, and biological systems can be viewed at:

> http://www.clarityconnect.com/webpages/-cramer/PictureIt/welcome.htm

Many subjects are covered on WWW Virtual Library. It also includes a useful collection of links to other sites:

> http://www.earthsystems.org/Environment/shtml

Index